Success in School

Colette O'Connor

ROUNDSTONE

Published in 2012 by Roundstone, Ireland.

A CIP catalogue record for this book is available from the British Library.

An LCCN catalogue record for this book is available from the Library of Congress.

ISBN 978-0-9570505-0-1

Disclaimer And Information

The suggestions in this book are of a general nature. Any person using the suggested strategies needs to exercise his or her judgment to ensure that the activity is safe for the individual child. Avoid carrying out any of the strategies in this book that are uncomfortable for the child. Caution is particularly advised where there is an underlying injury or medical condition. If in doubt consult a health-care practitioner who knows the child. Neither the author nor the publisher accept responsibility for readers who implement strategies in an unsafe way or for the children involved.

If a child's attention levels remain poor after trying these strategies, it is recommended that a medical practitioner would assess him.

In this book, you will find examples of how to apply the suggestions provided. They are based on the author's experience of working with many children, parents and teachers. Fictional characters were used as examples to protect client confidentiality.

*Dedicated to all pediatric occupational therapists,
particularly those whom I have had the honor
of learning from and working with.*

Acknowledgements

Thanks first and foremost to all the parents, teachers and children I've worked with over the years. Next, thanks to all of the occupational therapists who I've had the privilege of learning from and working with. Thanks also to all my other colleagues, past and present, from whom I've learned so much. I'm grateful for the insightful editorial input by Nancy Grossman at Back Channel Press. Thanks to all my friends and family for their support and encouragement. In particular, thanks to Rachel Kissane and Brid Riordan for feedback on the first draft of this book and to Claire Gleeson, Angela Kearney and Yvonne Higgins for helpful references. Special thanks to Cathal, my wonderful husband, for his love and willingness to share my attention with the writing of this book.

Contents

Part I

The Facts

Chapter 1
Is This Book For You?

What is this book about?

This book is about helping kids improve their focus for learning. In it, you'll find easy ways to help make this happen that won't result in a battle of wills. The goal is to make learning more enjoyable for children by helping them to concentrate. The methods outlined do not require extra time or money. In fact they usually make life easier for both the adult and child.

Step one in learning is to pay attention. In this book, the terms "pay attention," "concentrate" and "focus" are all used to mean the same thing: the ability to do or listen to one thing while ignoring other things. Listening to the teacher and ignoring what's happening outside the window. Ignoring the sound of voices or TV coming from another room while doing homework. Settling down to be able to be attentive. If a child needs to learn something at home or at school, first he needs to focus on that information. By helping children pay attention, adults can help them learn.

Few adults realize how using the senses can help children to pay attention. Fewer still know that there are *seven* senses, not five. This book uncovers the two "secret senses" and explains the powerful effect they have on kids' concentration.

There are many myths about how children should learn. Most adults believe at least one of them, even those adults who have been teaching for years. Often, it is these myths that stop kids from learning to their potential. This book aims to bring to light these myths.

Once the secret senses and myths have been explained, practical strategies for improving kids' attention will be outlined. These activities are suitable for use both during class and at home addressing homework. They give parents and teachers a variety of ways to help kids to focus on learning.

Who is this book for?

This book is for anyone who helps children learn, either at home or school. This includes parents who help their kids with homework and teachers with big classes of children. In this book children are referred to as "he" and "him." Of course, all of the information also applies to girls! The term parent is used to cover all caring situations. The guidelines given are particularly suited to children aged four to eleven. However, much of the information could be applied to older kids and even adults.

This book is deliberately short because people with children in their lives tend to be very busy. If you want key facts and practical strategies presented in a concise way, this book is for you.

Most children have difficulty in concentrating on learning at least some of the time. Teachers and parents often need to help them to focus on what they are doing. This book provides easy and effective ways for adults to do that. If a child's attention remains poor after trying them, it is recommended that you have a medical practitioner assess him.

If you are thinking of using these strategies with a child who has a diagnosis or injury that affects his everyday life, first check with his health-care practitioners. None of the strategies in this book will cure a condition, but they can make it easier for kids to concentrate, and can be used along with whatever else helps.

Are you a parent helping with homework?

During homework, does your child ever experience or do any of the following?

- Have difficulty concentrating.
- Get up out of his seat to roam around the room.
- Pick things up and fidget with them.
- Look around the room instead of at his work.
- Frequently want things such as food, drink, or a different pencil.
- Seem giddy or overactive.
- Slump on the chair.
- Seem too tired for homework.
- Move on his chair, perhaps rocking or wriggling in his seat.
- Sit in odd positions such as kneeling or hanging off the chair.
- Talk about distant sounds that you don't even notice.
- Complain about everyday smells such as the dinner cooking.
- Chew or suck on things that should not be put in a child's mouth.
- Not look at you when you ask him a question.

If you recognize any one of the above, this book can help you and your child. You may try to tell your child that if he would stop and just get on with his work, he could have it done in half the time. No matter how often you remind him, however, he continues with the same behaviors.

This can be very frustrating for a parent who is trying to help a child to learn. You'll find easy ways to overcome these difficulties and get kids to pay attention in this book.

Are you a teacher?

If you teach one child at a time, you may see similar behaviors to the ones listed above. If you teach a classroom of children, these difficulties may be multiplied.

Does a child you teach do any of the following?

- Look everywhere in the room except at you, the teacher.
- Make noise with things such as rattling his pencil case.
- Rock in his chair, fall off his chair or rarely sit still.
- Lie across the desk or sit in unusual positions.
- Chew on things, maybe to such an extent that you worry that he will choke.
- Complain about ordinary sounds, like those of children singing or a clock ticking.
- Complain about smells that no one else notices, such as polish on the desk.
- Use every excuse to get up from his desk, like needing to use the restroom.

Ways to deal with each of the behaviors listed above are contained in the following chapters. Teaching can be made difficult by these kinds of behaviors. Even if the teacher can tolerate them, other children in the class may find them annoying and distracting. They can lead to rows between children.

You, as a teacher, may worry about a child's lack of concentration. You know that if a child is not listening to what you're saying, he cannot learn from you. It can be a huge challenge to get every child in the classroom to listen to you.

No doubt you've already developed many successful strategies to deal with this. However, if you're anything like most teachers, you're always on the lookout for more.

What's different about this book?

This book looks at the subject from a fresh angle. It is written by an occupational therapist who has specialized in a subject called "sensory processing." Sensory processing has a huge impact on learning but most people have never heard of it. Knowing about sensory processing gives adults new tools to assist children to focus on learning. Sensory processing is explained in a way that is clear and easy to understand in the next chapter.

You will find other facts that are not commonly known about child development in this book. Up to now, this information has not been available to most parents and teachers. The material may, therefore, be new to you even if you already know lots about helping children to learn.

Adults I work with frequently find that coming to understand these aspects of children's behaviors greatly helps. It can allow the parent or teacher to prioritize where to put his or her energy. Adults become clear on which behaviors they should ignore in children and which they need to address. I have worked with many parents and teachers who have found that even one simple change can greatly reduce stress.

Children who have been helped

Many children have already been helped by the information contained in this book. I've known children who engaged in a wide variety of unconventional behaviors in class or while doing homework. They chewed on clothing, rulers, pencils, erasers, pencil cases, their fingers and paper. They ended up with wet clothing because they sucked on it so much.

They found every possible reason to get up from their seats. When on their chairs they were in constant motion, rocking their chairs or hanging off them. Their heads were often buried in their schoolbags. They knelt on their chairs or lay across their desks.

They picked up everything near them. They shook these items, rattled them, pulled on them, or put them to uses for which they'd never been intended. In doing so, they made noise, disrupted the classroom and broke things. They threw things at other kids, either on purpose or by mistake. They ended up with all kinds of strange things in their pockets such as adhesive putty or stones. Some constantly wanted to touch other children's hair or clothes.

Some children I work with get very upset when they have been touched lightly by another child. They claim that they have been hurt, for example, when someone walks past and brushes against them. Some are nervous of moving in certain ways. Others are constantly on the go.

I work with children who hate writing and resist doing it. Written work takes many times longer than it should. They have had such a negative experience of writing that they are no longer willing to try. They have established bad handwriting habits that they are unable or unwilling to change.

Many teachers and parents have successfully addressed the types of difficulties listed above through the information in this book. Explanations for and strategies to address these behaviors are to be found in the chapters that follow.

How to use this book

Most children do not need all the strategies given in this book. Some kids can learn better by using just one. Think of this book as a menu of strategies from which you can choose as you wish. The best way to know whether a strategy will be useful is to try it out.

It is possible to use the strategies successfully without understanding the secret senses and how they work. I have found, however, that adults are more likely to try these strategies once they understand how they help children's brains. For this reason, the facts behind the strategies will be explained first.

The examples given explain how the information provided can be put into practice. It is important to take note of the safety information contained in boxes throughout the book.

Chapter 2
The Secret Senses

As will be explained in this chapter, the senses are essential in helping children pay attention. Most people think there are only five senses: seeing, hearing, touching, tasting and smelling.

In fact there are two other senses that have a huge effect on our everyday lives. They are like air, in that they are invisible yet necessary. These senses are a basic part of life, but most people don't know they exist. They play a central role in helping children to focus on learning.

Senses and the brain

Before looking at the secret senses, it helps to be clear about how all senses work. Bodies are made up of tiny cells. There are many types of cells with different jobs to do. Some cells have the job of picking up information about sensations. For example, the eyes have cells whose job it is to gather information about what can be seen.

When the cells in the eyes collect this information, they send it to the brain. This point is important, because the brain is the *control center* for everything that goes on in the body. The brain sorts out the messages received from the eyes and makes sense of them. In order to see properly, both the eyes and brain need to be working well.

It is useful to think of the brain as an interpreter of sensations. It's like being in a foreign country where you don't speak the language. You can see the people talking and you can hear what they're saying, but you have no idea what it means. You need someone else who can interpret for you. The interpreter translates what you are hearing into a language that makes sense to you.

Similarly when you are at home listening to others, your ears are taking in the sounds but it is your brain that is acting as interpreter, making sense of what you are hearing.

Different parts of the brain have different jobs. It's possible for somebody's brain to work perfectly except for a tiny little part. The job of this part might be to make sense of what the eyes see. If this part isn't working, the person might be blind. This could be the case even if his eyes themselves are working perfectly.

This is true for all senses. To taste something sweet or salty, the cells in your mouth and your brain must both be working properly. To smell a flower, cells in both your nose and your brain are involved. To be able to feel somebody's touch requires reactions from both your skin and the part of your brain that responds to touch. Your skin needs to be able to feel the touch and to send a message to the brain. Your brain needs to interpret being touched in order for you to feel the sensation.

This interpreting job that the brain does is known as "*sensory processing*," and it goes on inside everyone all the time. Without the brain doing this job, you would not be able to see, hear, taste, smell or feel. The eyes, ears, nose, mouth and skin are all sending information to the brain, and these senses affect other activities in the brain.

Sensation and learning

Everyone knows that brains have a role in learning. Not everyone realizes that sensations do too. This is because of the connection between the brain and the senses described above. At the same time that we are busy learning, our brains are busy sorting through sensations. This includes everything that we are seeing, hearing, smelling, tasting and/or feeling.

When the brain does a good job, we are not consciously aware of all of the sensations our brain is processing. This is because our brain tells us what we need to focus on and what we can ignore.

14

The brain can be thought of as a director in one's personal movie. It decides what to focus on and how it fits with the overall story. For example, if a student is sitting in a classroom, his brain may tell him to concentrate on the voice of the teacher. It may tell him to ignore sounds of air conditioning, coughing, background chatter and traffic outside.

Many situations typically include background noises. Most people can filter them out without noticing. They take this ability for granted. Others, however, are unable to filter out background sounds and can become very distracted by them. This may seem obvious for the sense of sound. It may not be so obvious when it comes to the secret senses.

WHAT ARE THE SECRET SENSES?

The two secret senses can be thought of as the senses related to movement. They are called the *vestibular* and *proprioceptive* senses, and are explained below.

THE VESTIBULAR SENSE

Where is it?

The cells that are responsible for the vestibular sense are in the inner ear, in the part of the ear that is inside the head. All movement of the head involves the vestibular sense.

What does it do?

The cells in charge of the vestibular sense take in two types of information. The first thing they do is to notice every time the head moves. They notice the intensity and direction of the movement. This is the sense that allows a baby to feel being gently rocked from side to side. It is the sense that results in dizziness after being spun around in a fairground ride.

The second thing that these cells do is to notice gravity. They spot the difference between standing up straight and hanging upside down. They tell the individual which way he is turned in relation to the ground.

What happens when it doesn't work properly?

When the vestibular sense doesn't work properly, the person may have a poor sense of gravity. He may dislike tilting his head backwards, which may give him a frightening sensation of falling. A child who has problems with his vestibular system may be able to spin himself lots but never get dizzy. It may result in a child either wanting to be always on the move or having low energy levels.

What difference does it make?

The vestibular sense has an impact on everyday life in a variety of ways. The most important for the purpose of this book is its effect on concentration. This sense affects how alert you are.

People know this instinctively even if they have never heard of the vestibular sense. Slow, gentle rocking tends to make people sleepy. That's why people do it to calm a baby, and why there are rocking chairs.

On the other hand, fast movement where the head is turned in lots of directions is stimulating. People do not generally get sleepy on rollercoasters! Fast movements tend to energize people more than slow ones. The greater the variety of directions that the head is moving in, the more the movement physically stimulates the person.

Some people find certain types of movements too stimulating and may become frightened or sick. They may develop motion sickness or be afraid of some fairground rides.

If someone is tired, a brisk walk might wake him up. If a child has used fast equipment in a playground, he may become giddy and over-excited. Providing the right balance of movement can help to get people into a calm and alert state, the state that is considered to be ideal for learning.

When referring to this state in terms of the secret senses, occupational therapists often use the word "alerting"[1] to describe activities that are energizing. Alerting activities can energize children when they are sluggish. Calming activities are used when children are over-stimulated. Descriptions of such activities are to be found later in this book.

Individual differences

It is obvious that people have individual preferences when it comes to the vestibular sense. Some people love rollercoasters and others hate them. Some people find nothing more relaxing than exercise involving a great deal of movement, such as tennis. Others are not particularly active and would prefer to curl up on the sofa with a good book.

These preferences are based on real, physical differences between people. Everyone experiences the world in a slightly different way (some people in a very different way!).

If you have children, you know that individual babies may have different preferences in what movements they experience as calming. People need different levels of movement to function at their best.

What is its effect on learning?

The way in which a person moves affects how alert he feels. This obviously has an effect on his ability to learn. If he's sleepy he will not be able to concentrate on learning. If he's over-excited, he is also unlikely to be able to learn to the best of his ability.

As movement can change an individual's level of alertness, it can alter his ability to concentrate on learning. It can perk him up or calm him down, depending on the type of movement it is.

How to apply this concept will be outlined in later chapters. This knowledge can be used to help children get into the best state for learning.

Some children find it easier to learn when they can move. Although there are general trends, the type and frequency of movement may vary from child to child. It's possible to provide children with the type of movement that they need in order to learn, both in a classroom or during a homework session. It need not be disruptive.

On the contrary, it usually makes learning more enjoyable and effective. It can be incorporated fluidly into teaching so that no additional time or resources are required. The practicalities of how to do this will be discussed later in this book.

THE PROPRIOCEPTIVE SENSE

Where is it?

The cells responsible for proprioception are in muscles and joints. All movement involves proprioception.

What does it do?

Proprioception allows you to know where various parts of your body are without needing to look at them. If you close your eyes and can feel where your hands are, proprioception is at work. If you move your hand without looking at it and can still tell where it is, that's proprioception.

The proprioceptive sense is engaged by what is often called "heavy work." This happens when joints experience traction or compression. This comes about in a variety of everyday situations, when pushing, pulling, lifting, weight-bearing or stretching.

At the grocery store you might experience a variety of proprioceptive inputs. For example you might push and pull a grocery cart, stretch to reach something on a high shelf and lift bags of groceries.

A young child crawling on the ground experiences proprioceptive input, particularly through weight-bearing on his knees and hands. Holding your arm up, such as when polishing a window, provides good proprioceptive input. The more effort involved, the more proprioception the person is getting. Children who fidget are often looking for proprioception (see Chapter 8).

What happens when it doesn't work properly?

When proprioception isn't working well, an individual may need to look more at what he's doing. He may need to be able to see his hands in order to know what they are doing. When he cannot see his hands, for example when buttoning a top button, he may find the task difficult to perform. A child with poor proprioception may trip frequently. He may need to look at his feet to know where they are so that he doesn't fall.

What difference does it make?

Proprioception helps get people into a state in which they are both calm and alert. Many like to stretch soon after waking up in the morning. That action provides proprioceptive input, which can help you to wake up a bit.

Some people find the slow, sustained movements of stretching exercises to be relaxing. The good thing about proprioception is that it can help to perk you up when you're in a slump, or it can calm you down if you're feeling tense.

Individual differences

As with all of the senses, people differ in what works best for them. Some people love the intense proprioceptive input that they can get in a gym. They find that they can relax better after working out. Other people find that a stretch at their desk is all they need.

What is its effect on learning?

Together with the vestibular sense, proprioception has a role in affecting concentration levels. It is very useful to know about, as it can help to calm children who are overactive and over-excited. It can also help to perk up children who seem to be half asleep. This makes proprioception ideal to use with a group of children who have different needs. Easy ways in which proprioception can be used in teaching and learning will be outlined later in this book.

All learning is sensory

Sensation plays a vital role in learning. No learning takes place without sensations. When the two secret senses are included, everything in the world is experienced through the senses. Every single piece of information that people learn is taken in through one or more of their senses.

Everything learned is delivered to the brain from cells whose job it is to experience sensation. Sensations play a vital role in an individual's ability to concentrate on learning.

EXAMPLE: MOVEMENT AND LEARNING

Alex is a nine-year-old boy who had no difficulties at school. His parents felt embarrassed discussing their problem because nobody else saw it. They wondered if it was their fault.

When Alex came home after school he was like a whirlwind of energy. It seemed as though he made a huge effort to do what he was told during the school day. All of his pent-up energy was released as soon as he came home. They described him as "bouncing off the walls." They couldn't get him to sit for anything for more than a minute. During homework and dinner he was constantly up and down. They had tried giving him time to play outside after school to burn off some energy. Sometimes that seemed to make him worse.

It appeared that Alex had an intense need for movement. He repressed this during the day at school in order to fit in. Once he got home he could no longer contain himself.

His parents learned about the two secret senses involving two different types of movement. This began to shed some light on possible solutions.

When they gave him time to play outside, Alex often chose activities that provided lots of vestibular input. These involved fast head movements in different directions. He chose activities such as playing chase with his friends and bouncing on a trampoline. When it was explained that vestibular input can be stimulating, they realized that these types of play were making things worse.

Their solution was in proprioception (heavy work) because this type of input is never overly stimulating. Alex is very strong and so requires quite intense exercise for his age. His parents enrolled him in a children's gym class that involved learning strengthening exercises.

Alex's parents learned how to do warm-up and cool-down stretches with him. He learned exercises such as half press-ups and how to stand on his head against a wall. His parents put a chinning bar in a walk-in closet doorway at home. He doesn't use it for chin-ups, however. He holds it and hangs on it.

Alex's parents developed a routine of getting him to spend twenty minutes doing proprioception-based exercises before homework. This greatly improved his concentration. He is motivated to do the exercises because he likes the idea of having strong muscles. They still allow him to play outside with his friends, but they know that he needs calming proprioception-based exercises afterwards for concentration. Alex now gets homework done faster and more easily.

1.   Mary Sue Williams & Sherry Shellenberger, *TAKE FIVE! Staying Alert at Home and School* (Albuquerque: Therapy Works Inc., 2001).

Chapter 3
Sensory Processing Disorder

When interpretation of sensations goes wrong

When it comes to sensations, everyone is different. Within any group of people it is normal to have a wide variety of sensory needs and preferences. Although this book is mainly for kids with typical sensory processing and those working with them, it is good to be aware of how this can go wrong.

Some individuals' brains do not interpret the messages coming in from the senses correctly. When this happens, it is known as *sensory processing disorder*. This may be seen in a variety of ways.

For example, some kids might feel little or no pain when they get injured. On the other hand, a child may experience light touch as being painful in certain situations. As a result he may find it physically uncomfortable when somebody brushes lightly against him. He may be very fussy about the clothes he wears. He may like baths but dislike the feeling of a shower. He may eat only certain types of food.

It is useful to know that different cells are responsible for light and heavy touch. I have worked with many children who find it painful when someone lightly touches off them, but enjoy heavy touch sensation such as wrestling or being tackled on a football field. These children usually enjoy receiving firm, deep massage and giving tight hugs.

The secret senses – the senses of movement – may not be interpreted correctly by the brain. This generally results in the person either avoiding certain types of movement, or craving movement and being constantly on the go. I have met many children who are fearful of certain types of movement. Some avoid tilting their heads back when getting their hair washed. Many of the children I work with avoid swings or dislike going high on swings.

The children who crave movement often spin themselves repeatedly and never seem to get dizzy. Sometimes they prefer jumping and other intense movements. Some have a poor ability to judge where they are to the extent that they keep bumping into things.

Sensory processing disorder can occur either on its own or alongside other difficulties. Estimates suggest that one in twenty kids has a sensory processing disorder.[1] If you suspect that your child may be one, it is recommended that he be assessed by a practitioner experienced in the area. Occupational therapists with specialized training in sensory processing (also known as sensory integration) are qualified to identify this difficulty.

An in-depth discussion of sensory processing disorder is outside the scope of these pages. If you would like to learn more about it, please see the list of resources. If teachers are reporting that your child seems to have significantly more difficulties than would be expected at his age, it may be time to have him assessed by a health-care practitioner.

EXAMPLE: WHEN TOUCH HURTS

Sarah is a five-year-old girl who was having difficulties making friends at school. She complained about her classmates hurting her, even though there was no evidence to suggest this. Teachers had seen her get angry at classmates for what seemed like no reason. Occasionally she hit other children. She particularly disliked standing in line, and always wanted to be the first in line.

Sarah had no difficulties playing with her older brothers. One of her favorite activities was playing wrestling with them. She was very affectionate at home and loved tight hugs. Her parents were worried about her ability to socialize with people outside the family. They spoke to her often about how important it was to be nice to kids in her class. It made no difference.

Sarah's parents learned how light touch can be uncomfortable for some children. They realized that she became upset when someone touched her lightly. At first it was hard for them to understand how it hurt her when somebody brushed past her. After all, she enjoyed her brother lying on top of her when they played wrestling! They had thought that she really enjoyed being touched because she was so affectionate at home.

Sarah's parents had noticed that the touch she seemed to look for was deep pressure in the form of tight hugs. Without being aware of it, they had learned that she did not like light touch. Her family had automatically adjusted to her needs. At school this did not happen.

Once this was explained to Sarah's teacher, things at school began to improve. The teacher encouraged her to stay at the back of the line where she could have more space. This meant that it was less likely for other children to bump into her. The teacher told the class general stories about how it is important to accept differences in people. When necessary he explained to individual children that light touch hurts some people's skin.

At home her parents explained to Sarah that most people's skin is not like hers. It helped Sarah to understand that people didn't mean to hurt her. She learned to tell kids in class when they accidentally hurt her. She started to make friends at school. When they had the opportunity, her parents later brought her to an occupational therapist for further help.

1. Lucy J. Miller, *Sensational Kids: Hope and Help for Children with Sensory Processing Disorder* (New York: Penguin Group, 2006).

Chapter 4
Life Is Sensational

Experiencing the world differently

People assume that others' experience of the world is similar to theirs. In reality individuals' experiences can vary significantly. For example, some people easily hear or smell what most people don't notice. Others can be color blind for many years without realizing it. They may assume that everyone else sees red or green in the same way that they do. Similarly, some may have problems with the secret senses that people are unaware of.

It is worth bearing in mind how people differ in what they like when it comes to senses. For example, they may prefer to wear or decorate with different colors. When it comes to food, one man's feast is revolting to another.

Musical taste varies from calm and classical to noisy rock. People choose different scents of air fresheners. Some people prefer the feel of a bath, others a shower. It is fully accepted that there are individual differences when it comes to the five senses most commonly known.

Confusion arises, however, when it comes to what people prefer in the secret senses. Because these two senses are not generally recognized, some behaviors are not widely understood. This can lead to adults misunderstanding children's behavior in a learning situation.

Using sensations in everyday life

As explained previously, everything that people experience in the world is taken in through their senses. Everyone instinctively uses sensations to help them to get through the day in the best way they can. They just don't normally think about it in that way.

When people become aware of this, it allows them to actively choose sensations. This sets them up to be in the best possible state throughout the day. This awareness can also help adults to guide kids towards appropriate ways to use sensations. This can provide children with the tools they need to be able to focus on learning.

It's normal for individuals to like different sensations at different times of the day. You may choose a different volume or tempo of music in the morning compared with the evening. If driving, you may find that you switch off the radio when carrying out a more challenging maneuver, which requires a different level of concentration. The radio may perk you up and help you concentrate during a routine drive. When you need more concentration, a quiet environment may work better.

There may be a sight or sound in your home that you are unaware of while you are feeling calm. The same sight or sound, however, may become noticeable and irritating if you are tired or stressed. Children also have varying needs for and reactions to sensations throughout the day.

How people feel varies during the day. Most people start off with their energy levels on the low side. Without being aware of it, they use a variety of sensory strategies to help them to become more alert. They may use sounds, such as turning on a radio. They may use how something feels on their skin, like having a shower. They may use movement, such as going for a swim or a walk. They may alter how things look by turning on bright lights, or by starting off with dimmer lighting.

The taste and texture of the foods they eat and the flavor and temperature of what they drink also affect how they feel. They may prefer crunchy textures and chilled juices to get them going. If they want a more gentle start, they may choose something warm, smooth and sweet.

If they need to focus while sitting at a desk during the day, they may work better by getting up and moving when they feel sluggish, or having something to eat or drink at the desk. At a meeting, they may chew on a pen or fidget with paper clips, their hair or clothing. Many people need to maintain a clear and neat desk in order to concentrate, while others work effectively amid a pile of clutter. If sharing an office with somebody, they may discover that they have quite different preferences regarding lighting and background noise.

After a stressful day people have different ways of unwinding. Some people relax by exercising. Others find it more calming to curl up on the sofa for a while. Both are valid ways of de-stressing, and each reflects the differences in people's sensory preferences.

These choices that people make throughout the day are all based on real physical differences in individuals' bodies. They often unconsciously draw on activities that they instinctively know help them to function more effectively throughout the day. Adults have learnt this through experience. Children may need your guidance.

Sensory strategies

For the purpose of this book, the term "sensory strategies" is used to describe activities that provide the right type of sensation for a given situation. In later chapters you will learn more about which strategies are alerting and which are calming.

Through this knowledge you will be able to help a child in a slump to get more energy. You will likewise discover new ways to help a child who is over-stimulated to calm down.

When trying to get children to focus, it helps to first become aware of your own use of sensory strategies. You can do this by taking a couple of minutes to answer the questions below.

Comparing your answers to those of a friend can make for a revealing conversation. It can be interesting to notice how the sensory strategies that you use differ from those of people around you. It may be challenging if what you prefer differs from the preferences of those you live with!

Questions for sensory awareness

See the prompts on page 37 to help you to answer the following questions:

What types of sensations do you choose in the morning?

Sight

Sound

Touch

Taste

Smell

Proprioception

Vestibular

What types of sensations do you choose during the day?

Sight

Sound

Touch

Taste

Smell

Proprioception

Vestibular

What types of sensations do you choose in the evening?

Sight

Sound

Touch

Taste

Smell

Proprioception

Vestibular

Prompts

- Sight - What lighting do you prefer? Do you prefer the room to be clear or cluttered?

- Sound - Do you prefer noise or silence? What type and volume of music would you prefer?

- Touch - Would you prefer a bath or shower? Do you prefer the feeling of certain types or textures of clothes?

- Taste - Do you prefer different types of foods at different times of the day? Do you prefer strong or mild flavors? Smooth or chewy food? Hot or cold? Do you chew pens or gum?

- Smell - Are you aware of smells that you dislike first thing in the morning that don't bother you at other times of the day? Are there smells that you dislike that other people seem to like?

- Proprioception (involved in all movement) - When do you stretch? Do you like activities such as doing stretching exercises or working out with weights? Do you ever fidget? How do you feel after physically demanding housework? How do you feel if you are sitting down all day?

Prompts (cont'd)

- Vestibular (involved when your head moves) - Do you like to get exercise in the morning or do you prefer a slow start? Do you ever go for a walk or jog if you are feeling sluggish? Do you prefer to move quickly or slowly?

Children's use of sensation

Children often need to be taught appropriate ways to get the sensations that they need. There are many benefits to recognizing and providing for children's needs for sensations. Teaching and learning become more effective and less stressful. The child is more engaged and the whole experience becomes more enjoyable for everyone.

Young children naturally want to learn. Tapping into their sensory preferences allows them to learn in a way that they can be enthusiastic about. How to do that is explained in this book.

Using strategies with children

Frequently children instinctively do things to help themselves learn. On the other hand, if adults fail to recognize their attempts to pay attention for what they are, they can accidentally prevent these kids from learning.

As explained later in this book, the idea is not to let children do whatever they please. Rather, the aim is to recognize kids' attempts to concentrate. Adults can then guide them to do what is appropriate to the situation to help them to learn.

The strategies suggested in the following chapters are tools[1] to promote learning. They are neither toys nor treats. They should be used as part of learning; they are not to be used as rewards. Using them from the start of class or homework is important to avoid encouraging unwanted behavior in children. This will be discussed further in Chapter 16.

When you first try out the strategies, bear in mind that for kids, absolutely anything can be a distraction at first. Children have an endless capacity for wonder and curiosity. Remember, when you introduce something new, however boring it may seem, try it for a few days until the novelty wears off. Then decide on whether the strategy is helping the child to learn.

1. Diana A. Henry, *Tool Chest: for Teachers, Parents and Students Handbook* (Glendale: Henry Occupational Therapy Services, 2000).

Part II

The Myths

Chapter 5
Common Myths

Most people were brought up to believe certain ideas about paying attention in order to learn. These beliefs may seem so obvious that we never think to question them. The most common of these beliefs goes like this: the best way for children to learn is to sit still and look at either their work or their teacher.

In fact, this is not necessarily the case. Children paying attention can look quite different from what adults expect. As will be explained, sometimes children need to move and look away in order to concentrate. Problems arise when the adult does not understand what the child is doing or why he is doing it.

The adult in question may then try to get the child to conform to his or her version of what concentrating should look like – which can actually prevent the child from learning! Adults will often assume they can tell whether a child is paying attention just by looking at him. Frequently they're wrong because they base their judgment on what they were told when growing up.

Adults need to know all the facts when it comes to the subject of paying attention.

Times have changed

Getting kids to sit still for learning often worked better in the past because of the fear factor. There was a time, not so long ago, when children would do exactly what they were told because they were afraid not to. Of course, some children were able to easily meet adults' expectations. Those who couldn't often just gave up on learning, even if they were bright and had great potential. Thankfully, the way society deals with children in the classroom has greatly changed in the last few decades.

Children's needs in many areas are now recognized. The education system aims to tap into children's natural motivation for learning. Many lessons are enjoyable and fun for children, especially for those in younger classes. Parents and teachers widely rejoice that times have changed in this way. Both want education to be a positive experience for kids. A feeling lingers, however, that more tools and strategies are needed on how to manage children's behavior. Parents often wonder how strict they should be with their child. Some teachers fear losing control of the class by being too lenient. This book aims to better equip parents and teachers in helping children to pay attention for learning.

The myths

Listed below are some commonly held beliefs about learning. All children are different. For many typical, healthy, well-adjusted kids, one or more of the following statements is completely untrue. Where adults hold one or more of these beliefs, this can block children's learning. The myths are:

- You can tell by looking at a child whether or not he's paying attention.

- If a child is not looking at you, he's not paying attention to what you're saying.

- If a child is fidgeting, he's not listening.

- A child needs to sit still to learn.

- Eating, drinking and chewing are distractions from learning.

- The same learning environment works for all typical children.

- Learning and play are two separate things.

- There's no need to teach school-age children how to draw shapes.

- Children should start to learn handwriting when they're 4 or 5 years old.

These will be addressed individually in the following chapters. Some of what you'll find in this book may seem radical, maybe even unbelievable. It may be the exact opposite of what you were brought up to believe.

If this is the case, I'd ask you to simply try out some of the suggestions. And as I've said, it's important to continue them for at least a few days so that the novelty can wear off. *Then* check whether the child is learning. In my experience the result is usually a happier child who is learning better.

Chapter 6
Myth: You Can Tell By Looking At A Child Whether Or Not He's Paying Attention

EXAMPLE: WHICH STUDENT IS CONCENTRATING?

Let's take the example of a typical class. Most of the students are listening to what the teacher is saying. Bob is rocking on his chair, making noise. He has tried to get up to sharpen his already quite sharp pencil three times in the last ten minutes. He rarely looks at the teacher.

Mark is sitting properly on his chair, looking in the direction of the teacher. Many people glancing at this scenario would assume that Mark is paying attention and Bob is not.

The teacher, however, is wise enough to realize that this may not be the case. She asks a question and Bob answers it correctly. He has clearly been listening to what she was saying. She asks Mark the next question. He has no idea what she is talking about and obviously has not been concentrating. The teacher is concerned, however, that Bob's behavior is distracting other children in the class. She is also worried that he might actually fall off the chair and get hurt.

When Bob goes home his mother helps him with his homework. She spends most of the time trying to get him to sit properly on his chair. She firmly believes that he needs to be sitting still to learn. Bob becomes cranky and argues with her. She finds the whole experience very frustrating.

This happens every time Bob has to do homework, and his mother worries that it will have a negative effect on their relationship. However, she is more concerned about him getting a good education. Because of this, she continues to try to get him to sit still.

Asking questions

It's not always possible to tell by looking at a child whether or not he is paying attention. Believers in this myth will tell you that if a child is looking away, fidgeting and/or moving, he's not listening. I can't stress enough that this is not necessarily true. How each of these behaviors can actually *help* kids to learn will be explained in the following chapters.

The "You Can Tell By Looking" myth is the cause of much frustration in trying to get children to focus. It's so common that many people take it as fact – they fail to recognize it as a belief. Everyone has an image of how the perfect child looks when he's learning, and yes, some children conform to that image. Others, however, look very different when they are learning to their potential. One aim of this book is to influence the picture of learning that adults hold in their heads, in the hope that this will lead to more realistic expectations.

If children look distracted, the most effective way to check if they're paying attention is to simply ask a question. If a child can answer a question on whatever you've been talking about, obviously he's paying attention. This is true no matter how he appears, even if he's sprawled upside down on the couch and looking miles away. If he has no idea what you were talking about, then, yes, he was clearly not paying attention.

And, of course, many children can appear as though they are paying absolute attention while they are mentally replaying yesterday's football game. You can't assume that those kids sitting quietly and looking at you are mentally with you. The best – and only – way to find out is to ask a question.

Again, I am not suggesting that children should be allowed to do as they please. The strategies in this book are not meant to be an excuse for inappropriate behavior in children. There are ways to allow kids to do what they need to while following classroom and homework rules. These will be explained in later chapters.

Many parents and teachers I've worked with have found the information in this book to provide great relief. It allows them to let go of their preconceived ideas and long-held beliefs about how children should look when paying attention. It enables them to focus instead on whether the kids are learning.

Chapter 7
Myth: If A Child Is Not Looking At You, He's Not Paying Attention To What You're Saying

Different cultures

Many people believe that a child should look at them if they have asked him a question. In Western society people generally consider making eye contact a sign of respect. The belief is that this behavior provides concrete evidence to the speaker that he is being listened to.

Expectations around eye contact vary between cultures. Beliefs are opposite to those of Western society in many regions of Latin America, Africa and Asia,[1] where it is considered disrespectful, even challenging, to look at another individual directly in the eye.

This is particularly the case if a child is involved. In these cultures, it can be considered rude for a child to make direct eye contact with his teacher. In Japan, children are taught to look at the teacher's neck when communicating with him or her. Awareness of these differences is useful if you are interacting with children from cultures other than your own.

Looking away helps learning

There are also very practical reasons why a child from any culture might look away from you. Looking away plays an important role in learning.[2] We adults often tend to look away from the person we are in conversation with when we're thinking. Watch people's behavior.

For example, adults look away from the other person as they struggle to remember a name. And the more challenging the mental task, the greater the chance that eye contact will be broken. Again, watch people while they're trying to figure out a complicated answer. We often close our eyes, or look upwards or to the side.

There are various theories as to why people do this. Some writers suggest that looking at another's face can be distracting. They propose that when people are concentrating on one thing, it makes it easier to shut out other distractions.

Others in the field have associated various eye positions with different types of mental activity.[3] Their research suggests that we turn our eyes in certain directions when doing certain mental tasks. The directions usually remain the same for any one particular person, although they may vary between individuals. For example, people often look up and to their left when trying to remember how something looked. On the other hand, they often look to their right when trying to imagine how something might sound.

Do some research of your own. You can learn a lot by watching people's eye movements when you ask them different types of questions. Whatever the reason, there is agreement that looking away can be a sign that the person is thinking.

But there's more. Research has shown that adults give more correct answers when they are allowed to look away.[2] They tend to perform worse if they are asked to maintain eye contact with the speaker. People also speak less fluently if they have to look continuously at the other person.

Looking away is a skill that develops in childhood. As they get older, children start to look away more while trying to figure out an answer or trying to understand something. It is a sign of progress in a child's mental ability.

A study where younger children were encouraged to look away after they had been asked a question found that their ability to answer correctly actually improved.[2] It may, therefore, be worth encouraging children to look away from you while they are thinking.

Children who already have this skill look away most when they've been asked a challenging question. If a question is very easy for them, they can usually produce the answer without breaking eye contact. However, if the question is too difficult for them, they will typically continue to look directly at the questioner.

Looking away can be a sign that the question was just right – not too easy and not too hard. By observing these responses, adults can get a better idea of where they should pitch their teaching. It can provide clues to help them to know when they should step in to help a child.

Allow enough time

Most teachers recognize that children need to look away while they're thinking. It has been shown, however, that many underestimate the amount of time that a child might need.[4] It can be useful to remember that while he is looking away, he's probably still thinking. If he resumes eye contact with no answer, this is generally a sign that he's given up.

It may be worth waiting for a child to look at you before deciding if he can answer. If you are a teacher, consider that the next time you're faced with students looking away from you. It could be a sign that you're doing a great job and have a very attentive class!

1. Robert T. Moran, Philip R. Harris and Sarah Virgilia Moran, *Managing cultural differences: global leadership strategies for the 21st century* (Burlington: Butterworth-Heinemann, 2007), http://books. google.com/books/ (accessed March 19, 2011).

2. Fiona G. Phelps, Gwyneth Doherty-Sneddon and Hannah Warnock, "Helping children think: Gaze aversion and teaching," *British Journal of Developmental Psychology* 24 (2006), 577–588.

3. Joseph O'Connor, *NLP Workbook: A practical guide to achieving the results you want* (London: Element, 2002), 51.

4. Gwyneth Doherty-Sneddon and Fiona G. Phelps, "How teachers respond to children's eye gaze," *Educational Psychology* 27, no.1 (2007), 93-109.

Chapter 8
Myth: If A Child Is Fidgeting He's Not Listening

Fidgeting in the context of learning is when a child picks up something unrelated to the task that he's doing. He keeps it in his hand, maybe pulling on it, twisting it, or squeezing it.

At school when he is supposed to be listening to the teacher, he might pick up something – a pencil, pencil case, anything within reach. At home he might fidget with a mobile phone or remote control, pushing the buttons or scratching the surface. He may damage what he's fidgeting with by accident.

Why fidget?

Because it involves movement, fidgeting provides the sense of proprioception, the sense that can be either calming or alerting, as discussed in Chapter 2. It can, therefore, help both children who have too much and too little energy to concentrate, which is why fidgeting plays a very useful role in learning. Not all children need to fidget, but some really do in order to learn to the best of their ability.

Of course fidgeting must not distract other children, and it also mustn't distract the child doing the fidgeting. The solution is to give him something safe, quiet and boring to have in his hands. The fidget item should be thought of as a tool[1] to improve concentration, not a toy. Its purpose is not for play or entertainment. It's put in children's hands to enhance learning.

Caution is advised if you have in mind a child who tends to put things into his mouth. In this case, many of the items suggested for fidgeting will not be suitable. Give only items that are safe for oral use to kids who put things in their mouths (see Chapter 10).

The aim is to find something for the child that he can fidget with in an unconscious way. He should not find it interesting to look at, nor should his attention be focused on the fidget tool. His attention should be on listening to the teacher or whatever he's supposed to be doing.

A good fidget tool doesn't distract the child from learning. On the contrary, it improves the child's ability to *concentrate* on learning. For this reason the best fidget tools for learning quickly become visually boring, but remain interesting to hold and handle.

A sample fidget tool

My favorite fidget tool for homework or school is cheap and easy to come by. It's made from plain stockings or pantyhose. The legs are cut into loops one to two inches in width. One pair of stockings should provide you with enough fidget tools for an entire class.

You can learn a lot by allowing all the children in the class to have one. Kids who drop or lose their fabric may need to have it tied to their desk or chair at hand height.

Children can be told that holding a fidget tool can sometimes make it easier to listen. You'll find that the children who don't need to keep their hands busy while paying attention will soon lose interest. However, the children who need to fidget in order to concentrate could benefit greatly from this simple item.

As with all of the strategies in this book, introducing something new is often initially distracting. Allow a few days for the novelty to wear off. Then you can decide whether or not the tool is promoting learning.

Use the ideas in the previous chapters to judge whether or not it's helping the child. Kids are rarely distracted by a piece of fabric for long. Those who continue to use it usually do so unconsciously as it helps improve their concentration.

How to Make
a Fidget Tool

- Get stockings or pantyhose made out of relatively thick, plain fabric.

- Lay the legs out flat.

- Cut across the legs at intervals of roughly 1 to 2 inches. This should yield you a nice pile of short strips of fabric.

- Open up the strips to form loops. These are your fidget tools.

- For safety, the loop should not be big enough to fit over a child's head. You can knot the loops to make them smaller if necessary.

A school could have a recycling bin for pantyhose (clean of course!) that could supply free fidget tools for the entire school.

Other fidget tools

An alternative to a fidget loop could be a hair scrunchie, or an elasticized key chain or bracelet. Make sure that whatever is used is not so elastic that it could be employed as a slingshot, firing missiles across a classroom!

All children are different, of course. Some may prefer a different type of sensation to stretchy fabric. Be guided by their preferences. Some kids like something to hold and squeeze.

For homework, sponge balls (also known as stress balls) may be suitable, though I don't recommend these in general for school. If they're dropped in class, they tend to roll away, which is distracting. Also, balls are normally associated with play. Just so there's no confusion, fidget tools are for learning, not for play. If a stress ball is used at school, a good rule is that it must stay in a pocket.

Instead of a ball you could use a piece of foam for the child to squeeze. Another option is adhesive putty wrapped in plastic wrap. Avoid adhesive putty if it turns out that the child loves watching it as he pulls it. Remember, it's okay that a fidget tool feels interesting, but it shouldn't be visually interesting.

For some children the texture of the item may be more important. Many children feel calmed by feeling certain textures, from sandpaper to silk and everything in between! Involve the child in choosing a fidget tool. Use whatever works and is safe for the child. It's suggested that the child be allowed to use just one fidget tool for learning.

Doodling is a form of fidgeting. It can help kids to pay attention. Research has shown that doodling can help people to remember what they've heard.[2] Doodling involves scribbling or drawing in such a way that it requires very little attention. Because of this, most of the individual's concentration is available for learning. It's important to be aware of the difference between doodling and creating art, however. If drawing requires the person's concentration, it's no longer doodling.

Hard to believe

Allowing children to fidget can be a difficult concept for many adults to accept. You may have heard repeatedly as you were growing up that fidgeting is bad. To the contrary, many children I've worked with have been able to learn better with a fidget tool.

When they give it a try, most teachers and parents find the use of fidget tools liberating. They no longer waste time and energy trying to get individual children to stop fidgeting. Rather, they can focus on helping children to learn. If you're still in doubt, I can only suggest that you try it out and observe the results. Just make sure to allow a few days for any novelty factor to wear off.

EXAMPLE: FIDGETING THE RIGHT WAY

Ann was a five-year-old in her first year of school. By now most of her classmates had settled into the school routine. She continued to be very distracted during class. Her parents had tried giving her something to fidget with at school but this never worked out. It ended up being more of a distraction. She frequently dropped or lost the fidget tool. She became distracted by looking for it.

I suggested securely attaching a piece of stretchy fabric close by. It could have been attached either to the top of a leg of her chair or under the desktop in front of her. It was attached just under the desktop so that it was at an easy height for her to reach.

This greatly improved the situation, as her fidget tool was always there for her. She could use it whenever she needed to and it was no longer a source of distraction.

SAFETY NOTE: If the child you have in mind tends to put things into his mouth, the above items are best avoided for safety. Instead get something that has been designed for chewing (see Chapter 10).

Avoid giving items to young children to fidget with that could become missiles or weapons! Elastic bands and paper clips should be avoided as fidget tools in classrooms for this reason.

1. Diana A. Henry, *Tool Chest: for Teachers, Parents and Students Handbook* (Glendale: Henry Occupational Therapy Services, 2000).

2. Jackie Andrade, "What Does Doodling Do?" *Applied Cognitive Psychology* 24, no.1 (2009), http://www.big-doodles.com/downloads/study-about-doodling-jackie-andrade-fulltext.pdf (accessed March 26, 2011).

Chapter 9
Myth: A Child Should Sit Still To Learn

The previous chapter about fidgeting refers to children who can't keep their hands still. This chapter is about movements that are less subtle, where the child wants to move his whole body. He may constantly invent excuses to get up from his chair, especially the one teachers hesitate to refuse, needing to use the restroom. When he's sitting, he can rarely sit still. At home he may wander around the room instead of sitting down and then staying seated to do his homework.

Why move?

Do you know a child who's constantly moving around on his chair or has difficulty remaining seated? If so there's a good chance he's one of those children who needs to move in order to learn. As discussed in Chapter 2, movement is intrinsically linked with the ability to learn.

Different types of movement have varying effects on how alert people are. As we know, slow rhythmical movement generally tends to be calming and sleep-inducing. That's why, as I said, we have rocking chairs, not to mention gliders, hammocks and cradles, and why we rock babies to sleep.

In contrast, faster, more irregular movement can be alerting. If you want to stay awake and focused, a fast walk or jog may be just what you need.

When a child wriggles in his seat, this is often an instinctive reaction. Without realizing it, he may be trying to help himself focus. It can very well be an unconscious attempt to be better able to learn. It's important to recognize why a child is moving in the way he is.

Wobbly cushions

For school or homework, sitting on a cushion that allows a certain amount of movement can aid learning, providing enough movement to allow some children to concentrate better. To avoid children feeling self-conscious about their cushions, it's ideal to have a few available in class for those who want to use them.

A partially inflated camping cushion that's a bit wobbly can be very effective. Or try using a hot water bottle partially filled with cold water, ideally disguised inside a cushion cover to improve its appearance and limit joking. Specially designed "wobble cushions" are also available commercially (see Resources).

Whatever type of cushion you use, make sure that it's no bigger than the seat of the chair and that it won't slide off. Also ensure that the child's feet are firmly supported for safety. Brains can concentrate on learning better when bodies are firmly anchored by having feet supported. If the chair is too high for the child's feet to reach the ground, provide a footrest. A low stool or some telephone directories taped together can make good footrests.

SAFETY NOTE: If you provide a cushion, make sure that it is no bigger than the seat of the chair and that it will not slide off. Non-slip material should be used if required. Ensure that the child's feet firmly reach the ground or footrest. This also helps concentration.

Movement breaks

All children benefit from regular movement breaks. If you're a teacher, you've probably noticed the difference in concentration when children don't get enough exercise. Many teachers see a noticeable difference on days when the weather doesn't permit children to get outside to play. It's ideal to incorporate some kind of activity involving movement every 20-40 minutes to help children focus.

This doesn't have to disrupt work. Activities that involve lots of proprioception are best. As discussed in Chapter 2, this is calming for children who are restless and alerting for those in a slump. Some exercises can be done at their desks, or sitting on their chairs.

Two activities for classrooms that can be easily done without disrupting the class are chair push-ups and stretches (explained on pages 69 and 70). In addition to movement breaks, individual children can be given jobs to do involving physical activity, such as handing out books.

> *SAFETY NOTE: Do not carry out any activities that are uncomfortable for the child. Any physical activities carried out should be within his ability levels and should not be overly exerting. If in doubt about an individual child's abilities, seek advice from a health-care practitioner.*

Calming kids

Generally, fast movement tends to be stimulating. That's why children can be quite excitable after school recess or active play at home. If that's the case, do a few minutes of activities involving proprioception before starting class or homework. This sort of activity is also known as "heavy work." In the classroom, the chair push-ups and stretches previously mentioned are ideal. More ideas for homework are discussed below.

Generally, activities involving pushing, pulling, stretching and carrying are calming. Make sure that children don't carry anything heavier than is safe for them – recommended maximum weight that children should carry is usually considered to be 10-15% of their body weight.

Activities involving taking body weight through the arms, such as chair push-ups, are also calming. Another easy but useful exercise is to have the kids simply press the palms of their hands together for 30-60 seconds. The more physical exertion that is required, the more effective the activity tends to be. So after playtime and before work, try adding heavy work activities to your routine. These can be useful any time you need to calm children down.

> SAFETY NOTE: Children should not carry anything that is too heavy for them. Recommendations for the maximum weight a child should carry are generally 10-15% of the child's body weight.

Classroom movement breaks

On the following pages are my two favorite activities for classroom use. Chair push-ups are quick, easy, and equally involving for all children. Stretches, performed out of their seats, give students a little more time to work out the wiggles.

Chair Push-Ups

- Sit on a chair with your feet on the ground.

- Put your hands on the sides of the seat of the chair. If the chair has armrests, put your hands on these instead.

- Take your weight through your hands and lift yourself off the chair a few inches. Feet can stay on the ground. If you're strong enough, lift the feet too.

- Keep this pose, staying over the chair for 5-30 seconds, depending on your strength.

- Avoid bouncing quickly up and down as this could be over-stimulating for some.

- When ready, sit back on your seat.

Classroom Stretches

- Push back your chair and stand with the desk in front of you.

- Lift your arms out in front of you, then lift them up over your head.

- Lift your heels up from the ground.

- Stretch your arms and fingers up as high as they can go.

- Hold this posture for 5-30 seconds.

- Bring your arms down in front of you and hold them out in front of you.

- Return to a normal standing position with your arms by your sides.

The problem with sitting still

It may be obvious by now that telling a child to sit still can actually prevent learning. For some children, sitting still requires all of their concentration. If they manage it, they're lucky if they have any concentration left for learning.

Adults move around and fidget all the time. The difference is that they've learned to do so in subtle ways appropriate to the situations they're in. If they're in a meeting at work, they may pick up a paper clip or a pen. If they're in a lecture hall they shift in their seat regularly. Teachers move around the classroom.

Children tend to have a much more intense need for movement, and kids are too young to have learned what's socially acceptable in different environments. Because of this, they often get into trouble for moving and fidgeting in learning situations. Ironically, their bodies are seeking exactly what they need in order to learn. The problem is that adults often don't realize this. Instead, they try to prevent children from moving.

Appropriate behavior

Of course adults need to help children to fidget and move in ways that are appropriate. I'm not suggesting that kids should be allowed to do whatever they feel like.

Still, they can be taught and allowed to move in ways that won't disrupt class or homework.

Each child is different, and sitting still isn't necessarily the best way for a child to learn. I suggest that you try some of the different ideas in this book and see what works. Remember that anything new can be a distraction at first. Try a strategy for a few days before judging whether it's helpful.

More homework ideas

Before expecting them to do their homework, it's ideal to give children some time engaged in physical activity. This helps them to get ready to concentrate on learning. Parents also have a great opportunity for movement during homework. Ideas for activities just before and during homework are in the boxed text in the following pages.

When parents don't insist that their children remain seated for homework, the possibility for peaceful learning greatly increases. It may be necessary for the child to sit for part of his homework, for instance when working on his handwriting.

When his attention begins to fade, it may help him to move. He could learn to get up and jump 10 times beside the table before sitting down again to resume work. Select from the suggested calming and alerting activities, depending on whether your child is overactive or in a slump.

Spinning or twirling themselves can be good for children whose energy level is low, but do see the safety note below. Some children can be very sensitive to spinning so make sure they don't overdo it; the effect of spinning can last for hours.

Judge based on the reaction of the individual child. Some kids can spin lots with very little effect. Others can become overly energetic after a few spins. Avoid spinning if the child has epilepsy unless your doctor has said that it is safe. If your child has a sensory processing disorder, first see an occupational therapist. He or she can advise you on whether spinning is suitable for your child. Never spin a child who doesn't like it.

Children can literally move while learning, as well as taking movement breaks. For example, when children are learning things by rote they could walk in the room while reciting. This might be helpful while learning spelling or math tables.

As well as moving, using positions other than sitting can help children to pay attention. When reading, kids may concentrate best while kneeling or lying on their tummy on the floor. Again, it's worth experimenting with different types of movement and positions during homework. Try out anything new that you introduce for a few days. Remember to judge effectiveness by whether or not the child is learning.

Alerting Activities for the Home

If your child seems tired, these activities provide vestibular input which can perk children up. Select from the list.

- Jumping on the spot 10 times

- Twirling himself around 3 times (see safety note below)

- Jumping jacks

SAFETY NOTE: Spinning can be powerful and its effects can last for hours. It can make children nauseous and/or overactive. It should generally be avoided for kids who have epilepsy – please seek advice from your doctor. If your child has a sensory processing disorder, see an occupational therapist who has specialized in sensory processing. He or she can advise you on whether spinning is suitable for your child. Never spin a child who does not like it.

Calming Activities for the Home

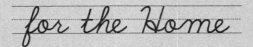

The activities below involve proprioception, which can be calming for children. Select from the list.

- Chair push-ups.

- Stretching up to the ceiling.

- Stretching out to the sides as if trying to touch the walls.

- Pushing against the wall, pretending to push it down.

- Marching on the spot, lifting knees up high.

- Household chores involving physical exertion. Some kids enjoy them! Suitable activities could include polishing windows, pulling wet clothes out of the washing machine or vacuuming carpets.

EXAMPLE: A TEACHER
ALONE WITH 30 CHILDREN

I spoke with a teacher who had 30 children in the classroom. She taught six- and seven-year-olds. Because none of the children had a diagnosis, she did not have an assistant in the classroom. Although she had many years of experience, she found this a particularly challenging group.

Several children in the class were very active and found it difficult to concentrate. These children took up much of her time. She worried that she was not able to give as much attention to the quieter students. She had heard about sensory strategies but felt that she could not implement them, as she was alone. Also, she had no budget with which to buy extra materials.

I encouraged her to introduce regular proprioception-based exercises during class. She didn't have much space in her room, so what she could do was limited. Every 20-30 minutes she got all her students to stand up and do classroom stretches. Then she told them all to sit down and do chair push-ups. I had told her to make sure to avoid children bouncing up and down in the chair. She was aware that this could be stimulating instead of calming.

The children enjoyed the activities and it seemed to have a generally positive effect on the class. When she noticed that some children were having a hard time listening to her, she suggested that whoever wished could do chair push-ups. She noticed that it was usually the kids who were having difficulty concentrating who chose to do them.

The teacher found this regime easy because she could do the same thing with everybody in the class. She knew that it would probably do them all some good, and certainly would not do any harm. She also did the activities herself and found that they had a calming effect on her. Overall it resulted in the class being easier to manage and her being less stressed.

Chapter 10
Myth: Eating, Drinking And Chewing Are Distractions From Learning

Why put something in your mouth?

Walk around any office area. Look at the pens and you'll find that many have been chewed. This is due to the simple fact that chewing and sucking can help us to think. They provide the sensation of proprioception.

Similarly, people often bring a cup of coffee to their desks. This is not just for a caffeine fix. The act of sipping a drink helps us to pay attention. Babies put their hands in their mouths. This helps to get them into a calm and alert state. Many parents have reported improved concentration when their child has something to chew or suck during homework.

What to put in your mouth

Lots of children can concentrate better if they're allowed to sip a drink or chew on something. Chewing is obviously better than fidgeting for written tasks, as the hands remain free for writing. In class, having something attached to the top of a pencil to chew may help. If a child is chewing a non-food item, ensure that it is safe for him to do so.

You'll find items specifically designed for children to put in their mouths under Resources. Several non-food items such as chewable jewelry and pencil tops are available. For homework, sucking on a sports bottle of water or having chewy or crunchy food at hand may aid concentration. Naturally, healthy foods such as sliced apples are preferable to empty calories. Again, see the safety note below.

Chewing gum can greatly help children to focus on learning, and two pieces are often better than one. It's been shown that chewing gum helps people to better remember what they read.[1]

There are lots of myths about the dangers of swallowing chewing gum, and parents are encouraged to investigate any concerns they might have before dismissing the idea of using chewing gum as a learning aide. Many parents have provided positive feedback on the use of chewing gum during homework time.

Too much sugar is obviously best avoided. Sugar-free chewing gum is available, as are natural options. You just want to make sure that they don't contain stimulants. Some children have no interest in chewing gum once the initial taste has worn off. For them chewing on a non-food item specifically designed for the purpose may work better. (Again, see Resources).

> SAFETY NOTE: Make sure that a child is able to safely chew and swallow all food given to him. If a child is chewing a non-food item, ensure that it is safe for him to do so. Items specifically designed for children to put in their mouths are recommended (see Resources). Please consult your dentist for any concerns related to teeth.

1. Lucy Wilkinson, Andrew Scholey and Keith Wesnes, "Chewing gum selectively improves aspects of memory in healthy volunteers," *Appetite* 38 (2002), http://www. wrigley.com/global/documents/scholey _appetite_study.pdf (accessed March 26, 2011).

Chapter 11

Myth: The Same Learning Environment Works For All Typical Children

It is human nature to assume that other people respond to everyday experiences the same way you do. In reality, what's needed in the environment to learn varies quite a bit from person to person. The sights, sounds and smells in a room can affect people in different ways.

Some children seem to have superhuman senses. I know children whose hearing is so sensitive that the sound of pencil points moving on paper during written work can bother them. I've also heard of children who were greatly upset when cleaning products at school were changed. Most people didn't notice, but these individuals found the smell sickening. It is important that adults respect these entirely real physical differences.

Sights

Most people work best in a clutter-free environment. Some children concentrate better when there is less to look at. In classrooms it's better to have colorful displays on the side and back walls. This leaves the area behind the teacher at the front of the room relatively free from distractions. Kids who lose attention more easily often work best sitting closer to the teacher. This is because there are fewer distractions, both moving and still, in their line of vision.

Some kids may benefit from a separate workspace at times when they need extra concentration, either a separate desk altogether, or by placing a divider around their work area.

Temporary dividers can be made easily from cardboard boxes. For example, an 18-inch square box with the top, bottom and one side cut out can be placed around the child's work area. The center section sits across the front of the desk and the two side sections wrap around the sides of the work space. A few of these could be available in class so that one child does not feel singled out. At home having a designated area for homework with a plain tabletop in front of a plain wall can help.

Good lighting can also enhance concentration. Many of us can recall how easy it was to lose attention in dimly lit lecture halls after lunch. A desk lamp for homework or class lights switched on during a dull day can make all the difference. Remember that what the adult would prefer is not necessarily what will work best for children. Try out various options.

Sounds

Different children can react differently to background noise. It's generally best to do homework in a quiet room with as few comings and goings as possible. You may be the type of adult who can work very easily with radio in the background, but bear in mind that we're all different. The sound of a radio might make it difficult for a child to learn.

On the other hand, it's quite possible that he will work *better* with some background music. The type of music itself can make a difference. Many people work better with classical music or similar instrumental music, finding only words distracting.

Music of a moderate tempo without too much variation in volume usually works well (Mozart is often suggested). It may be interesting for teachers to experiment with playing classical music in the background during some work periods.

Children who are greatly bothered by everyday sounds may need to be seen by an occupational therapist. They may need to be allowed to sit at a distance from the source of noise. Some may benefit from the use of noise protection headsets at certain times. Don't be fooled into thinking a child doesn't have problems with sounds just because he's noisy himself. Our own sounds don't bother us, in the same way that we can't tickle ourselves.

Many teenagers, however, will tell you correctly that they work better with loud rock music in the background. The teenage brain actually does seem to require more intense stimulation!

However, more familiar music generally serves best as a background. The novelty of something like radio with frequent commercial breaks tends to be more distracting. Usually the more effort that the task requires, the more calming the music should be. The best way to judge is to see if work is getting done and how long it's taking.

Smells

Don't dismiss a child's complaints about smells. If a child has a very sensitive sense of smell, he may find some common smells sickening, and sickening smells, needless to say, can make it difficult to concentrate on learning.

The sense of smell cannot be easily switched off. Unfortunately, it's not like being faced with something that you'd rather not look at. In that case you can close your eyes or look away. One solution can be to put cologne under the nose, as long as the child won't lick it off. The smell of polish on a school desk may really bother a child. If so, it may be worth experimenting to see if the child can concentrate better with a different cleaning product.

Likewise, during homework, some children find the smells of cooking very distracting. In this case it's worth trying out doing homework in a different room. As with anything new, it is important to commit to a trial period of a few days before judging effectiveness. Any change can be initially distracting until the child gets used to it.

Chapter 12
Myth: Learning And Play Are Two Separate Things

Play helps learning

Play helps children to learn. It helps their brains to develop. It lays the foundations needed for children to learn in school. When movement and textures are involved, play helps to develop sensory processing (explained in Chapter 2).

Using hands to dig and build in sand is an example of this kind of play. It's a symptom of modern life that adults may have to be conscious of children getting enough sensations. In previous generations, plenty of physical activity was part of everyday life. Children automatically felt a variety of textures through exploring nature.

Jean Ayres was an occupational therapist who did groundbreaking work on the link between sensations and the brain. She described sensations as being like food for the brain.[1]

In order for the brain to develop well, the body needs to experience plenty of sensations, including movement. Research by Ayres suggests that the ability for abstract reasoning is built on good sensory processing.[1] This is understandable when you consider that everything we learn is taken in through the senses.

Giving children the opportunity to move into and around play equipment promotes learning. Spatial ability, especially, is learned through movement. It also allows bodies to develop into strong anchors, needed for hands to work properly.

Physical activities, such as crawling and climbing, help to develop muscles in arms and hands. This allows children to do precise work with their hands. Messy play is great for exposing the skin to a variety of textures. This helps to stimulate the skin, important for the manual dexterity needed for tasks such as handwriting.

Getting kids moving

It goes without saying that sitting in front of a computer does nothing to help develop the kinds of sensory skills we're talking about here. However, these days some children are reluctant to do anything that doesn't involve a computer. In this case, it's worth exploring computer games that involve physical activity, such as simulated sports.

Schools can improve grades through fitness programs.[3] Studies show that kids who are physically fit do better academically.[2,3] In addition, they are less likely to need to be disciplined at school.[2]

Play that involves movement helps to get kids fit. Exercise has a positive effect on children's brains as well as their bodies, releasing chemicals in their brains that help kids to concentrate on learning.[3]

Giving kids a break

If you are a teacher, please avoid disciplining children by removing recess. School recess is an important opportunity for kids to get experiences that they need for learning. It is frequently counter-productive to deprive children of their break. If there is no alternative, supervised exercise during recess is suggested. There is great value, however, in unstructured free time for children. Research indicates that their attention for school work is better after recess.[4] It may take some kids a few minutes to settle back after the break, but it still helps their overall ability to pay attention.

It is common for children's attention to deteriorate after 40-50 minutes of school work. This may happen more quickly for some children, especially the younger they are. The longer the delay before recess, the worse students' concentration generally becomes.

Educators in Japan know this. There is great wisdom in the structure of elementary school days in Japan. Classes are usually 40-45 minutes long, followed by recess of 10-15 minutes, in addition to a longer break for lunch. Japan has a highly successful education system by international standards.*

In one study, Japanese teachers found it unbelievable that kids in America might only have one or two recesses a day.[5] Children's attention in school in Japan is generally excellent. The researchers contrasted this with the wandering attention they frequently observed in American classrooms. Having 10-15 minutes of play every 40-45 minutes is thought to help Japanese children focus on their schoolwork. Similar timing may be helpful for homework. Use of a visual timer can help kids to see when the next break is coming (see Resources).

Left to their own devices, children are often good at seeking out the types of experiences they need in order to learn. The danger is that adults will put them sitting at desks too early and for too long, thereby depriving them of the play opportunities they need in order to concentrate and learn.

*According to reports from the Organization for Economic Co-operation and Development (OECD).

1. A. Jean Ayres, *Sensory Integration and the Child* (Los Angeles: Western Psychological Services, 1998).

2. Texas Education Agency, "Physically fit students more likely to do well in school, less likely to be disciplinary problems," TEA News Releases Online (March 2009), http://www.tea.state.tx.us/news_release.aspx?id=21474- 90622&menu_id=692 (accessed March 26, 2011).

3. John J. Ratey, *Spark: The Revolutionary New Science of Exercise and the Brain* (New York: Little, Brown and Company, 2008).

4. A.D. Pellegrini, Patti D. Huberty, and Ithel Jones, "The effects of recess timing on children's playground and classroom behaviors," *American Educational Research Journal* 32(4) (1995), 845-864.

5. Harold W. Stevenson and Shin-Ying Lee, "Contexts of Achievement: A Study of American, Chinese and Japanese Children," *Monographs of the Society for Research in Child Development* 221, (55, 1-2) (1990), 1-107.

Chapter 13
Myth: There's No Need To Teach School-Age Children How To Draw Shapes

You may have noticed by now how many different ways a child's ability to pay attention for learning can be influenced. Here's another one. In order for children to pay attention for the purpose of learning, they need an appropriate level of challenge. It's a mistake to ask them to learn something that's far beyond the stage they're at.

We adults often expect young children to learn things that are too difficult for them, both at home and in the classroom. We may have the best of intentions. At home, we want to feel we are, to the best of our ability, preparing children to go out into the world. In the classroom, it can be particularly challenging if a good percentage of the students is functioning at one level, though others have yet to reach that point. Pay attention the next time you over-challenge a child. If you do, you'll see that he quickly loses focus because the task is too difficult.

Teaching shapes

Children need to learn how to draw basic shapes. This important skill is a foundation for learning handwriting. If handwriting is started before shapes have been taught and mastered, it may be hard for children to pay attention as the tasks expected of them grow more difficult.

Adults often take drawing shapes for granted, but learning this skill is a complicated task for kids. Some shapes are easier than others. In fact, there's actually a recognized developmental sequence for learning to draw shapes,[1] as illustrated in the diagram on the following page.

Kids generally learn to draw shapes in this order, although it's not unusual for left-handed children to learn the diagonal lines in the opposite order. Looking at shapes from this point of view, triangles are pretty tricky and come later.

It obviously makes no sense to attempt to teach children how to write "A" if they have yet to master drawing a triangle. Yet this is what happens in many homes and schools, to everybody's frustration. It's not fair to kids to teach them handwriting before they have learned how to draw shapes.

Diagram: Teaching Order for Drawing Shapes[1]

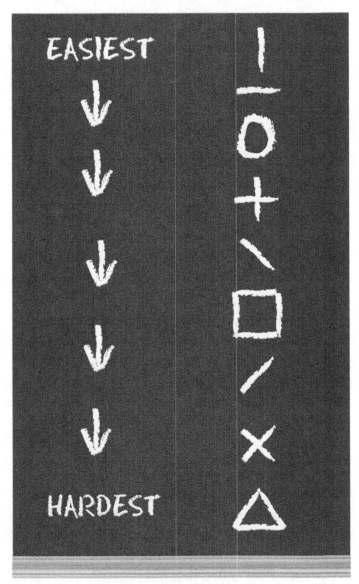

Imitation and copying

Imitation and copying are two separate steps in the learning process.[2] Imitation involves drawing what you have just seen someone draw. Copying a shape involves drawing it by looking at a pre-drawn shape, from a book, for example. For children, the ability to imitate someone drawing comes before learning to copy.

When learning to draw a triangle, the first step is imitating the actions of someone drawing a triangle. The next step is to copy a picture of a triangle without having seen how it was formed.

When you're teaching a shape, first show the child how it is done and allow him to imitate you. When he has a really solid grasp of imitating, show him a pre-drawn picture of the shape. Let him practice copying it until he has a solid grasp of that skill. Each shape should be worked on in this way before moving on to the next shape. This may sound boring to you, but repetition is how children learn best.

Introducing variety

Of course kids need some variety too. Changing the way in which shapes are practiced can provide this.[2] Shapes can be drawn in different colors, with pencils, crayons or chalk. They can be drawn huge or tiny. They can be drawn on a chalk board or a magnetic drawing board.

They can be drawn on lined paper, graph paper, blank paper or in a pocket notebook.

When he's working with pencils and crayons, make sure the child doesn't get into the habit of using a bad pencil grip. Habits are very difficult to change later. If he's not ready to hold the pencil well, using crayons and pencils one inch long (excluding the pencil point) can prevent bad habits from developing.

There are also plenty of ways to practice drawing without pencils. Kids can blow mist onto the car window and draw with their fingers. They can finger paint. Drawing in sand is popular. Spreading shaving foam onto wall tiles at bath time and drawing in the foam can be great fun.

The variety of ways shapes can be practiced is endless. Adults, through the use of variety, can facilitate children's ability to focus on a task – in this case, learning a shape – until it's mastered.

1. Keith E. Beery and Natasha A. Beery, *Beery-Buktenica Developmental Test of Visual-Motor Integration, 5th Edition* (Toronto: Multi-Health Systems Inc., 2006).

2. Marsha D. Klein, *Pre-Writing Skills* (San Antonio: Therapy Skill Builders, 1996).

Chapter 14
Myth: Children Should Start To Learn Handwriting When They're Four Or Five Years Old

When to write?

Children learn in a specific sequence, where one step builds on the previous step. Studies on child development show that certain skills are learned at certain ages. Some 4- and 5-year-olds are ready to learn handwriting. However, the reality is that most 4- and 5-year-olds are *not* ready to tackle this skill. For many children of this age, asking them to write is the equivalent of asking babies to stand before they can sit.

I can't stress this enough: it's normal for some children to learn to write later than others, just as children learn to walk at different ages. It's no problem for one child to learn to walk a few months before or after another does. It doesn't mean that either of them will be any better at walking when they are older! Likewise, a child might learn to write later than his friend. He can still be just as good as his friend at writing when they too are older.

When children start to put pencil to paper, the first shapes they learn are vertical and horizontal lines.[1] Next, they figure out how to draw circles. Because of this, the first letters that children are ready to learn are those involving these shapes.

Children may be ready and able to tackle letters such as E and O from an earlier age. It takes longer to be ready to learn more complex letters such as those involving diagonal lines. When a child has mastered copying a triangle, as explained in the previous chapter, he's probably ready to learn to write all the letters of the alphabet.

There are detailed statistics on children's abilities to copy shapes.[1] On average, about 50 percent of children aged 5½, and the majority of younger children, cannot copy a triangle. On their sixth birthdays, approximately one in five kids is still not able to copy a triangle. That's an average of four kids in each group of twenty of that age who aren't yet ready to write the more complex letters. In Finland, children usually start to learn to write when they are seven, so it comes as no surprise that Finland has one of the most successful education systems in the world.[2]

The dangers of too early a start

There are problems associated with trying to teach children to write before they're ready. As we've seen, children usually have great difficulty paying attention to a task that's beyond them.

This, in turn, can be both demotivating and demoralizing for them. It's like expecting an adult to be fluent in a foreign language on day two of a language course. It can destroy forever a child's interest in learning anything that involves handwriting. Such a child can be burdened for life with a negative attitude about all written tasks.

Secondly, children who are forced to learn before they're ready tend to develop bad handwriting habits. I have met many children with handwriting difficulties due, I believe, to having started to learn writing too soon.

I have seen terrible pencil grips that can't be changed because the habit has become fixed. I have met children who are extremely negative about writing even though they are fully capable. These are the children who've developed a negative association with handwriting from learning too young.

Even though they later develop the ability, they never learn well because they've believed from the start that they aren't good at writing, or just *can't* write. The truth is that they were forced to write years before they were ready.

In my experience, bad writing habits may be impossible to change and may indeed last a lifetime. These bad habits really make their presence felt later in children's school life, particularly when children need to learn cursive writing or to write quickly. The solution is to prevent this problem before it can start. The key is teaching children how to draw shapes *first*.

The joy of waiting

There's much to be gained by our understanding the sequence in which children learn to draw and write. Parents stop worrying that their five-year-old can't write. Teachers stop coming under unrealistic pressure from parents about writing.

Once teachers and parents know the importance of first teaching shapes, stress is reduced for all – for both children and the adults in their lives. When children are ready to learn to write, there are great teaching tools out there that provide structured lesson plans covering all the steps in the best order (see Resources).

Prevention, of course, is the best cure when it comes to bad handwriting habits. If it's too late for that, it may be worth seeking the advice of an occupational therapist to address handwriting difficulties.

1. Keith E. Beery and Natasha A. Beery, *Beery-Buktenica Developmental Test of Visual-Motor Integration, 5th Edition* (Toronto: Multi-Health Systems Inc., 2006)

2. Ellen Gamerman, "What Makes Finnish Kids So Smart?" The Wall Street Journal Digital Network, (February 29, 2008), http://online.wsj.com/article/SB1204253556561997.ntml#articleTabs%3Darticle (accessed July 10, 2011).

Chapter 15
Bringing It All Together

Many parents and teachers find that small, simple changes can make all the difference. Many find that they're better able to help children focus when they have the information in this book. Some children may benefit from using one suggestion. I have worked with a great many children, however, who need several at the same time.

EXAMPLE: CONCENTRATION PROBLEMS

David is a sweet seven-year-old, eager to please adults. In spite of trying his best, he found it difficult to concentrate during school and homework. He wasn't disruptive in class, but his teacher was worried because she felt that he was not learning to his potential. She saw that he was having concentration difficulties. His parents took him to a doctor and were told that he did not have ADHD (attention deficit hyperactivity disorder).

David's parents and his teachers tried out various sensory strategies until they found those that work best for him. He now sits on a wedge-shaped Move 'n' Sit™ cushion. It's a bit wobbly so he can easily move while sitting without making noise or distracting others. He needed a foot rest as his feet were dangling when he sat on the chair. His teacher taped together two old telephone directories and uses these to support his feet.

At school David keeps a loop of stretchy fabric in his pencil case. When he needs to listen to the teacher he pulls on the loop, winding it around his fingers. He has a Chew Ease™ pencil top (see Resources) pushed onto the top of his pencil. He finds that it helps him to think when he chews on this. His parents are happy that he is no longer chewing the paint from his pencil.

David now sits close to the front of the room, directly facing the teacher. She has removed art displays from the wall behind where she usually stands. There's not much behind her to distract him. She has also ensured that the children sitting beside him are not particularly noisy. She often gives him jobs that involve getting up from his desk, such as collecting up homework or helping decorate a bulletin board.

David's father helps him with homework every evening. He used to get David to do his homework straight after school, sitting at the table. Now he gives his son 20 minutes to play on the trampoline before starting homework.

For written homework, David sits at a table. He has a small stool under the table so that, again, he has something firm to rest his feet on. The patterned tablecloth has been replaced with a plain one. The table has been moved so that he can sit facing a plain wall.

When David is doing homework that does not involve writing, he doesn't sit at the table. When he is learning his spelling words, he walks around the room with the book in his hands. When reading, he lies on his tummy on a rug. He puts the book on the floor in front of him and props himself up using his arms.

David continues to need prompting from the teacher during school and his father during homework. However, he has been greatly helped by the use of these strategies.

Chapter 16
What About Behavior?

Good behavior

Understanding sensory processing is not meant to be an excuse for inappropriate behavior in children.[1] The aim is to improve, not avoid learning. Normal methods of encouraging good behavior should be employed, such as using praise and rewards.

For example, it's appropriate for parents to say something like "you can play after homework." They may also find it useful to use sensory strategies during homework. Trial and error and adult judgment may be needed to figure out the best sensory strategies.

As discussed in Chapter 12, children may need breaks to play for 10-15 minutes every 40-45 minutes. Apart from that, it's usually a mistake to completely remove children from their work to use strategies.[1]

Kids are smart! They'll quickly learn that if they act like they can't concentrate, they'll get to avoid their work. The solution is to build relatively boring sensory strategies into their learning. Ideally, this involves choosing a sensory strategy that can be used at the same time as work. Alternatively, the child could take a break for a minute in his chair or at his desk.

EXAMPLE: FIXING MISTAKES

Kate is a 10-year-old girl whose energy seemed to evaporate when it came time for homework. She very much enjoys being active. Her favorite activity is rollerblading. After a few minutes of sitting to do homework she became sluggish and almost sleepy. Homework dragged on for a long time due to her low energy levels.

Kate's parents had heard that movement breaks during homework can help children to concentrate. They noticed that she seems much more energetic when she is on the move. She is delighted when doing fast rollerblading. They started to let her play outdoors for 15 minutes when they saw her slump during homework (often every 10 minutes). However, this had few beneficial effects and homework time was dragging on longer.

Kate's parents came to me for advice. I explained that it was a bad idea to allow her outdoors so frequently during homework. She very much enjoyed getting out there. Without meaning to, in a way they were rewarding her with a treat when she wasn't doing her work. This was giving her no reason to get her work done. To the contrary, it could have tempted her to do poorly during homework so that she could get outside to play.

I advised Kate's parents to use movement to help her concentrate during homework in a different way. I suggested that they give her time to play outside before and after homework. They had already learned that the vestibular sense can be energizing (see Chapter 2). That's why they had been letting her go out during homework. I encouraged them to introduce activities that would provide vestibular sensation while doing homework.

For example, Kate could jump while learning things by heart. When reading they found that she performed better when walking around the room with her book. Her writing was best when she was seated, but she usually lost concentration after a few minutes of this.

I suggested that after those few minutes of writing, she should stand beside the table and jump or spin herself (see the safety note below). After a minute, she should sit back down and continue writing. This type of movement break was not exciting enough to tempt her to deliberately do poorly during homework. It was not a game. It was an active tool to help boost her attention.

Kate's concentration was still very poor when sitting to do written homework. Her parents found that they needed to get her to stand up and move every five minutes, but they made sure to keep her in the room and get her to sit back down after a minute. In spite of all the movement breaks, it took much less time to get homework done.

SAFETY NOTE: Remember, spinning can be powerful and its effects can last for hours. It can make children nauseous and overactive. It should generally be avoided for kids who have epilepsy – please seek advice from your doctor. If your child has a sensory processing disorder, see an occupational therapist who has specialized in sensory processing. He or she can advise you on whether spinning is suitable for your child. Never spin a child who does not like it.

From the beginning

It's important to put strategies in place before the child loses attention in order to benefit from them.[1] These strategies are tools to be used to promote attention, not as rewards or punishments.

For example if you're using chewing gum to help a child to concentrate, provide it from the start. Don't wait until you see the child losing attention. Otherwise, you run the risk of teaching a child to lose attention. Even if you do not intend to use the strategy as a reward, the child may experience it as that. Introducing it after a decrease in his attention may translate to the child that he gets something nice after losing concentration.

If you don't use these tools while the child's attention is still good, you might accidentally encourage him not to pay attention.

Homework

If a child needs a movement break during homework, he could stand beside the table and jump. After ten jumps, he could sit down again to resume work. Do not send him outdoors for what might be perceived as enjoyable play activities. Homework is not the time for practicing his footwork for soccer or riding his bike around the block.

Those activities are great for after school and before homework. They may even be suitable during a play break if homework lasts longer than 40 minutes. During homework, however, it's important to be careful not to make sensory strategies too much fun. If you do, it may lead to the child deliberately avoiding his work. If a child really needs sensation, he doesn't need it as a toy or favorite game.

For homework, movement can happen at the same time as learning. A child can walk or jump while learning spelling words – and without leaving the room. Homework may be most effectively carried out using a variety of positions, such as kneeling at a low table. For some children this may be more effective than sitting all the time. Handwriting is usually best if a child is sitting with his feet on the floor or a footrest. For reading and learning by rote, though, it's worth experimenting with options other than sitting.

In the classroom

As teachers know, one of the strongest rewards for young children is getting attention from adults, and whether it's perceived as either positive or negative doesn't matter. In a classroom situation, it's important that children using sensory strategies are not seen by their classmates as getting extra attention from the teacher.[1] Otherwise you may end up with a classroom of kids asking to use them purely to get the teacher's attention.

The easiest way to overcome this is to make sensory strategies available to everyone, then to comment as little as possible on them once they're in use. Usually the children who don't need them soon lose interest.

When children are using these strategies, they may need to be reminded about them. Take the example of a child who is starting to fidget with a noisy pencil case. He may need to be told to use the quiet fidget tool that's been agreed on. Remember, it takes everyone, children and adults alike, time to develop new habits.

If several children in a class are using fidget tools, it may be helpful to give general reminders. You could say "Children must be quiet when the teacher is speaking. If you need to keep your hands busy, use your fidget tool." Reinforce the fact that it's just one clearly identified item that each child is allowed to fidget with (see Chapter 8).

Don't make sensory strategies so much fun that kids act up just so that they get to use them.[1] Where possible, build strategies into the work (see Chapter 9). For the child who needs to move, let him sit on a wobbly cushion. Also, get him to do class-appropriate jobs such as gathering up materials. If it seems like several children in the class could do with some movement, take a couple of minutes to do some in-chair or at-desk exercises. Just remember – when it comes to sensory strategies for learning, boring is best!

1. Betty A. Paris and Carolyn Murray-Slutsky, *Is It Sensory or Is It Behavior?* (San Antonio: Psychcorp, 2005)

IMPORTANT POINT TO REMEMBER

WHERE SENSORY STRATEGIES ARE USED, THEY SHOULD BE PUT IN PLACE RIGHT FROM THE START OF THE CLASSROOM OR HOMEWORK SESSION. THESE ARE TOOLS TO BE USED TO ENHANCE ATTENTION FOR LEARNING. USING THEM AS REWARDS OR PUNISHMENTS IS COUNTER-PRODUCTIVE.

Conclusion

The ideas contained in this book can make school and homework easier, more enjoyable and more effective. If you'd like to discuss your individual situation, I am available by telephone or Skype (see www.success-in-school.com). Questions can be emailed to me through the Web site.

Sometimes just a change in perspective can make a difference. Dropping one or two of the myths that most people grew up believing can improve a situation.

There's no need to take my word for it. The suggestions outlined are fast, simple and free to implement. I'd encourage you to try them out for a few days. They have already been helpful to many parents, teachers and children. I hope that this book makes a positive difference to you and the children in your life.

Resources

Personal advice

The author is available to address individual queries. Please see www.success-in-school.com for details.

Products

No incentive or reimbursement was sought or gained for listing the products below. In my experience you may find them helpful.

- Move 'n' Sit™ cushions.

- Chew Ease™ pencil topper.

- Chewelry™: chewable wristbands and necklaces.

- Toys that involve jumping. One example is the Bungee Jumper™ toy, which is foam, much easier than a pogo stick and can be used indoors.

- Time Timer™: designed so that it's easy for kids to see how much time remains for a task, even if they don't understand numbers.

Suggested Books and Manuals

Sensory processing disorder

Lucy J. Miller, *Sensational Kids: Hope and Help for Children with Sensory Processing Disorder*. New York: Penguin Group, 2006.

Strategies for attention

Diana A. Henry, *Tool Chest: for Teachers, Parents and Students Handbook*. Glendale, CA: Henry Occupational Therapy Services, 2000.

Mary Sue Williams & Sherry Shellenberger, *TAKE FIVE! Staying Alert at Home and School*. Albuquerque, NM: Therapy Works Inc., 2001.

Handwriting

Janice Z. Olsen, *Handwriting Without Tears Kindergarten Teacher's Guide*. Cabin John: Handwriting Without Tears, 1998.

What's Next?

You might like more people to know about the information in this book. If so, you can help to spread the word by writing a review on www.amazon.com or www.amazon.co.uk.

You can help improve future editions of this book by sending the author your questions or comments at www.success-in-school.com.

Index

About The Author

Colette O'Connor has almost 20 years of experience as an occupational therapist. She specializes in working with children, many of whom have attention difficulties and conditions that impede learning. She has a particular interest and postgraduate education in sensory processing. With her background she brings a fresh perspective to education. In this book she shares her knowledge and experience to help kids focus on learning.

She lives in Ireland with her husband. She is available for telephone or Web-based consultation. She can also be contacted by email through her Web site, www.success-in-school.com.

CPSIA information can be obtained
at www.ICGtesting.com
Printed in the USA
BVOW08s1342191117
500832BV00001B/8/P